SUBTRACTION 3RD GRADE MATH ESSENTIALS

CHILDREN'S ARITHMETIC BOOKS

PROFESSOR GUSTO
EDUCATIONAL & INFORMATIVE BOOKS FOR CHILDREN
(PRE-K / K-12)

WORKSHEET NO. 1

Show your solution in the space provided below.

1. 30 - 22 =

2. 44 - 9 =

3. 49 - 2 =

4. 38 - 7 =

5. 39 - 6 =

6. 58 - 14 =

7. 53 - 8 =

8. 37 - 19 =

WORKSHEET NO. 2

Show your solution in the space provided below.

1. 29 - 22 =

2. 27 - 20 =

3. 51 - 5 =

4. 51 - 22 =

5. 52 - 7 =

6. 57 - 17 =

7. 36 - 15 =

8. 53 - 18 =

WORKSHEET NO. 3

Show your solution in the space provided below.

1. 39 - 4 =

2. 43 - 15 =

3. 31 - 18 =

4. 50 - 4 =

5. 25 - 22 =

6. 44 - 16 =

7. 29 - 20 =

8. 37 - 16 =

WORKSHEET NO. 4

Show your solution in the space provided below.

1. 56 - 19 =

2. 40 - 13 =

3. 36 - 22 =

4. 44 - 13 =

5. 42 - 10 =

6. 47 - 18 =

7. 37 - 23 =

8. 40 - 5 =

WORKSHEET NO. 5

Show your solution in the space provided below.

1. 56 - 25 =

2. 60 - 7 =

3. 27 - 9 =

4. 59 - 13 =

5. 29 - 24 =

6. 28 - 16 =

7. 25 - 19 =

8. 28 - 8 =

WORKSHEET NO. 6

Show your solution in the space provided below.

1. 57 - 25 =

2. 54 - 4 =

3. 53 - 16 =

4. 41 - 24 =

5. 56 - 23 =

6. 54 - 9 =

7. 30 - 6 =

8. 44 - 19 =

WORKSHEET NO. 7

Show your solution in the space provided below.

1. 39 - 15 =

2. 43 - 19 =

3. 51 - 17 =

4. 91 - 30 =

5. 50 - 31 =

6. 83 - 39 =

7. 79 - 36 =

8. 76 - 23 =

WORKSHEET NO. 8

Show your solution in the space provided below.

1. 72 - 44 =

2. 75 - 36 =

3. 81 - 18 =

4. 59 - 19 =

5. 63 - 15 =

6. 91 - 44 =

7. 50 - 39 =

8. 94 - 27 =

WORKSHEET NO. 9

Show your solution in the space provided below.

1. 80 - 14 =

2. 78 - 41 =

3. 77 - 44 =

4. 88 - 10 =

5. 53 - 35 =

6. 88 - 10 =

7. 66 - 42 =

8. 77 - 40 =

WORKSHEET NO. 10

Show your solution in the space provided below.

1. 53 - 11 =

2. 71 - 40 =

3. 86 - 19 =

4. 69 - 41 =

5. 52 - 25 =

6. 85 - 13 =

7. 88 - 22 =

8. 94 - 26 =

WORKSHEET NO. 11

Show your solution in the space provided below.

1. 63 - 21 =

2. 71 - 38 =

3. 89 - 21 =

4. 81 - 29 =

5. 53 - 45 =

6. 61 - 13 =

7. 61 - 15 =

8. 90 - 10 =

WORKSHEET NO. 12

Show your solution in the space provided below.

1. 71 - 28 =

2. 97 - 45 =

3. 61 - 20 =

4. 91 - 12 =

5. 81 - 44 =

6. 81 - 10 =

7. 55 - 22 =

8. 75 - 18 =

WORKSHEET NO. 13

Show your solution in the space provided below.

1. 72 - 45 =

2. 60 - 13 =

3. 87 - 42 =

4. 75 - 43 =

5. 84 - 49 =

6. 86 - 25 =

7. 97 - 30 =

8. 94 - 32 =

WORKSHEET NO. 14

Show your solution in the space provided below.

1. 90 - 48 =

2. 133 - 24 =

3. 134 - 18 =

4. 98 - 34 =

5. 135 - 14 =

6. 135 - 20 =

7. 87 - 39 =

8. 139 - 42 =

WORKSHEET NO. 15

Show your solution in the space provided below.

1. 149 - 59 =

2. 109 - 49 =

3. 137 - 41 =

4. 127 - 15 =

5. 125 - 25 =

6. 101 - 53 =

7. 138 - 25 =

8. 79 - 59 =

WORKSHEET NO. 16

Show your solution in the space provided below.

1. 79 - 61 =

2. 120 - 11 =

3. 94 - 31 =

4. 86 - 64 =

5. 129 - 26 =

6. 86 - 24 =

7. 129 - 56 =

8. 122 - 16 =

WORKSHEET NO. 17

Show your solution in the space provided below.

1. 119 - 49 =

2. 129 - 33 =

3. 141 - 46 =

4. 90 - 50 =

5. 138 - 21 =

6. 86 - 32 =

7. 84 - 24 =

8. 146 - 59 =

WORKSHEET NO. 18

Show your solution in the space provided below.

1. 143 - 63 =

2. 113 - 56 =

3. 89 - 33 =

4. 145 - 12 =

5. 106 - 51 =

6. 130 - 29 =

7. 83 - 62 =

8. 87 - 26 =

WORKSHEET NO. 19

Show your solution in the space provided below.

1. 143 - 11 =

2. 128 - 38 =

3. 99 - 42 =

4. 78 - 50 =

5. 82 - 60 =

6. 142 - 28 =

7. 192 - 22 =

8. 172 - 20 =

WORKSHEET NO. 20

Show your solution in the space provided below.

1. 154 - 104 =

2. 226 - 13 =

3. 211 - 55 =

4. 227 - 39 =

5. 226 - 43 =

6. 188 - 37 =

7. 176 - 81 =

8. 156 - 48 =

WORKSHEET NO. 21

Show your solution in the space provided below.

1. 239 - 101 =

2. 153 - 23 =

3. 174 - 114 =

4. 178 - 40 =

5. 197 - 82 =

6. 237 - 77 =

7. 227 - 17 =

8. 205 - 27 =

WORKSHEET NO. 22

Show your solution in the space provided below.

1. 217 - 31 =

2. 154 - 94 =

3. 236 - 80 =

4. 160 - 48 =

5. 153 - 100 =

6. 206 - 102 =

7. 174 - 100 =

8. 153 - 111 =

WORKSHEET NO. 23

Show your solution in the space provided below.

1. 234 - 71 =

2. 150 - 56 =

3. 156 - 34 =

4. 204 - 90 =

5. 208 - 98 =

6. 240 - 112 =

7. 171 - 117 =

8. 227 - 80 =

WORKSHEET NO. 24

Show your solution in the space provided below.

1. 203 - 112 =

2. 227 - 83 =

3. 244 - 89 =

4. 227 - 26 =

5. 185 - 21 =

6. 178 - 84 =

7. 152 - 81 =

8. 157 - 23 =

WORKSHEET NO. 25

Show your solution in the space provided below.

1. 175 - 97 =

2. 171 - 89 =

3. 175 - 70 =

4. 250 - 47 =

5. 218 - 63 =

6. 245 - 20 =

7. 209 - 70 =

8. 231 - 114 =

WORKSHEET NO. 26

Show your solution in the space provided below.

1. 188 - 50 =

2. 238 - 59 =

3. 249 - 69 =

4. 196 - 117 =

5. 220 - 64 =

6. 153 - 14 =

7. 226 - 65 =

8. 210 - 49 =

WORKSHEET NO. 27

Show your solution in the space provided below.

1. 197 - 37 =

2. 186 - 101 =

3. 163 - 10 =

4. 152 - 116 =

5. 181 - 108 =

6. 227 - 43 =

7. 248 - 41 =

8. 181 - 65 =

WORKSHEET NO. 28

Show your solution in the space provided below.

1. 194 - 39 =

2. 205 - 85 =

3. 180 - 23 =

4. 156 - 53 =

5. 250 - 111 =

6. 156 - 76 =

7. 198 - 110 =

8. 208 - 36 =

WORKSHEET NO. 29

Show your solution in the space provided below.

1. 182 - 85 =

2. 230 - 53 =

3. 214 - 53 =

4. 155 - 95 =

5. 163 - 46 =

6. 204 - 111 =

7. 224 - 189 =

8. 231 - 133 =

WORKSHEET NO. 30

Show your solution in the space provided below.

1. 266 - 176 =

2. 243 - 158 =

3. 293 - 151 =

4. 294 - 162 =

5. 291 - 163 =

6. 262 - 107 =

7. 240 - 106 =

8. 210 - 119 =

WORKSHEET NO. 31

Show your solution in the space provided below.

1. 261 - 161 =

2. 258 - 128 =

3. 253 - 172 =

4. 273 - 107 =

5. 266 - 88 =

6. 203 - 129 =

7. 259 - 173 =

8. 258 - 161 =

WORKSHEET NO. 32

Show your solution in the space provided below.

1. 280 - 199 =

2. 293 - 83 =

3. 292 - 183 =

4. 208 - 103 =

5. 270 - 77 =

6. 273 - 123 =

7. 241 - 169 =

8. 237 - 149 =

WORKSHEET NO. 33

Show your solution in the space provided below.

1. 222 - 169 =

2. 271 - 122 =

3. 286 - 177 =

4. 292 - 183 =

5. 210 - 77 =

6. 279 - 98 =

7. 290 - 198 =

8. 239 - 79 =

WORKSHEET NO. 34

Show your solution in the space provided below.

1. 226 - 150 =
2. 263 - 104 =
3. 266 - 194 =
4. 293 - 160 =
5. 213 - 77 =
6. 229 - 163 =
7. 251 - 138 =
8. 265 - 128 =

WORKSHEET NO. 35

Show your solution in the space provided below.

1. 205 - 127 =

2. 291 - 123 =

3. 210 - 170 =

4. 201 - 178 =

5. 210 - 83 =

6. 214 - 151 =

7. 255 - 110 =

8. 298 - 119 =

ANSWERS

1) 30 - 22 = 8
2) 44 - 9 = 35
3) 49 - 2 = 47
4) 38 - 7 = 31
5) 39 - 6 = 33
6) 58 - 14 = 44
7) 53 - 8 = 45
8) 37 - 19 = 18

1) 29 - 22 = 7
2) 27 - 20 = 7
3) 51 - 5 = 46
4) 51 - 22 = 29
5) 52 - 7 = 45
6) 57 - 17 = 40
7) 36 - 15 = 21
8) 53 - 18 = 35

1) 39 - 4 = 35
2) 43 - 15 = 28
3) 31 - 18 = 13
4) 50 - 4 = 46
5) 25 - 22 = 3
6) 44 - 16 = 28
7) 29 - 20 = 9
8) 37 - 16 = 21

1) 56 - 19 = 37
2) 40 - 13 = 27
3) 36 - 22 = 14
4) 44 - 13 = 31
5) 42 - 10 = 32
6) 47 - 18 = 29
7) 37 - 23 = 14
8) 40 - 5 = 35

1) 56 - 25 = 31
2) 60 - 7 = 53
3) 27 - 9 = 18
4) 59 - 13 = 46
5) 29 - 24 = 5
6) 28 - 16 = 12
7) 25 - 19 = 6
8) 28 - 8 = 20

1) 57 - 25 = 32
2) 54 - 4 = 50
3) 53 - 16 = 37
4) 41 - 24 = 17
5) 56 - 23 = 33
6) 54 - 9 = 45
7) 30 - 6 = 24
8) 44 - 19 = 25

1) 39 - 15 = 24
2) 43 - 19 = 24
3) 51 - 17 = 34
4) 91 - 30 = 61
5) 50 - 31 = 19
6) 83 - 39 = 44
7) 79 - 36 = 43
8) 76 - 23 = 53

1) 72 - 44 = 28
2) 75 - 36 = 39
3) 81 - 18 = 63
4) 59 - 19 = 40
5) 63 - 15 = 48
6) 91 - 44 = 47
7) 50 - 39 = 11
8) 94 - 27 = 67

1) 80 - 14 = 66
2) 78 - 41 = 37
3) 77 - 44 = 33
4) 88 - 10 = 78
5) 53 - 35 = 18
6) 88 - 10 = 78
7) 66 - 42 = 24
8) 77 - 40 = 37

1) 53 - 11 = 42
2) 71 - 40 = 31
3) 86 - 19 = 67
4) 69 - 41 = 28
5) 52 - 25 = 27
6) 85 - 13 = 72
7) 88 - 22 = 66
8) 94 - 26 = 68

1) 63 - 21 = 42
2) 71 - 38 = 33
3) 89 - 21 = 68
4) 81 - 29 = 52
5) 53 - 45 = 8
6) 61 - 13 = 48
7) 61 - 15 = 46
8) 90 - 10 = 80

1) 71 - 28 = 43
2) 97 - 45 = 52
3) 61 - 20 = 41
4) 91 - 12 = 79
5) 81 - 44 = 37
6) 81 - 10 = 71
7) 55 - 22 = 33
8) 75 - 18 = 57

1) 72 - 45 = 27
2) 60 - 13 = 47
3) 87 - 42 = 45
4) 75 - 43 = 32
5) 84 - 49 = 35
6) 86 - 25 = 61
7) 97 - 30 = 67
8) 94 - 32 = 62

1) 90 - 48 = 42
2) 133 - 24 = 109
3) 134 - 18 = 116
4) 98 - 34 = 64
5) 135 - 14 = 121
6) 135 - 20 = 115
7) 87 - 39 = 48
8) 139 - 42 = 97

1) 149 - 59 = 90
2) 109 - 49 = 60
3) 137 - 41 = 96
4) 127 - 15 = 112
5) 125 - 25 = 100
6) 101 - 53 = 48
7) 138 - 25 = 113
8) 79 - 59 = 20

1) 79 - 61 = 18
2) 120 - 11 = 109
3) 94 - 31 = 63
4) 86 - 64 = 22
5) 129 - 26 = 103
6) 86 - 24 = 62
7) 129 - 56 = 73
8) 122 - 16 = 106

1) 119 - 49 = 70
2) 129 - 33 = 96
3) 141 - 46 = 95
4) 90 - 50 = 40
5) 138 - 21 = 117
6) 86 - 32 = 54
7) 84 - 24 = 60
8) 146 - 59 = 87

1) 143 - 63 = 80
2) 113 - 56 = 57
3) 89 - 33 = 56
4) 145 - 12 = 133
5) 106 - 51 = 55
6) 130 - 29 = 101
7) 83 - 62 = 21
8) 87 - 26 = 61

1) 143 - 11 = 132
2) 128 - 38 = 90
3) 99 - 42 = 57
4) 78 - 50 = 28
5) 82 - 60 = 22
6) 142 - 28 = 114
7) 192 - 22 = 170
8) 172 - 20 = 152

1) 154 - 104 = 50
2) 226 - 13 = 213
3) 211 - 55 = 156
4) 227 - 39 = 188
5) 226 - 43 = 183
6) 188 - 37 = 151
7) 176 - 81 = 95
8) 156 - 48 = 108

1) 239 - 101 = 138
2) 153 - 23 = 130
3) 174 - 114 = 60
4) 178 - 40 = 138
5) 197 - 82 = 115
6) 237 - 77 = 160
7) 227 - 17 = 210
8) 205 - 27 = 178

1) 217 - 31 = 186
2) 154 - 94 = 60
3) 236 - 80 = 156
4) 160 - 48 = 112
5) 153 - 100 = 53
6) 206 - 102 = 104
7) 174 - 100 = 74
8) 153 - 111 = 42

1) 234 - 71 = 163
2) 150 - 56 = 94
3) 156 - 34 = 122
4) 204 - 90 = 114
5) 208 - 98 = 110
6) 240 - 112 = 128
7) 171 - 117 = 54
8) 227 - 80 = 147

1) 203 - 112 = 91
2) 227 - 83 = 144
3) 244 - 89 = 155
4) 227 - 26 = 201
5) 185 - 21 = 164
6) 178 - 84 = 94
7) 152 - 81 = 71
8) 157 - 23 = 134

1) 175 - 97 = 78
2) 171 - 89 = 82
3) 175 - 70 = 105
4) 250 - 47 = 203
5) 218 - 63 = 155
6) 245 - 20 = 225
7) 209 - 70 = 139
8) 231 - 114 = 117

1) 188 - 50 = 138
2) 238 - 59 = 179
3) 249 - 69 = 180
4) 196 - 117 = 79
5) 220 - 64 = 156
6) 153 - 14 = 139
7) 226 - 65 = 161
8) 210 - 49 = 161

1) 197 - 37 = 160
2) 186 - 101 = 85
3) 163 - 10 = 153
4) 152 - 116 = 36
5) 181 - 108 = 73
6) 227 - 43 = 184
7) 248 - 41 = 207
8) 181 - 65 = 116

1) 194 - 39 = 155
2) 205 - 85 = 120
3) 180 - 23 = 157
4) 156 - 53 = 103
5) 250 - 111 = 139
6) 156 - 76 = 80
7) 198 - 110 = 88
8) 208 - 36 = 172

1) 182 - 85 = 97
2) 230 - 53 = 177
3) 214 - 53 = 161
4) 155 - 95 = 60
5) 163 - 46 = 117
6) 204 - 111 = 93
7) 224 - 189 = 35
8) 231 - 133 = 98

1) 266 - 176 = 90
2) 243 - 158 = 85
3) 293 - 151 = 142
4) 294 - 162 = 132
5) 291 - 163 = 128
6) 262 - 107 = 155
7) 240 - 106 = 134
8) 210 - 119 = 91

1) 261 - 161 = 100
2) 258 - 128 = 130
3) 253 - 172 = 81
4) 273 - 107 = 166
5) 266 - 88 = 178
6) 203 - 129 = 74
7) 259 - 173 = 86
8) 258 - 161 = 97

1) 280 - 199 = 81
2) 293 - 83 = 210
3) 292 - 183 = 109
4) 208 - 103 = 105
5) 270 - 77 = 193
6) 273 - 123 = 150
7) 241 - 169 = 72
8) 237 - 149 = 88

1) 222 - 169 = 53
2) 271 - 122 = 149
3) 286 - 177 = 109
4) 292 - 183 = 109
5) 210 - 77 = 133
6) 279 - 98 = 181
7) 290 - 198 = 92
8) 239 - 79 = 160

1) 226 - 150 = 76
2) 263 - 104 = 159
3) 266 - 194 = 72
4) 293 - 160 = 133
5) 213 - 77 = 136
6) 229 - 163 = 66
7) 251 - 138 = 113
8) 265 - 128 = 137

1) 205 - 127 = 78
2) 291 - 123 = 168
3) 210 - 170 = 40
4) 201 - 178 = 23
5) 210 - 83 = 127
6) 214 - 151 = 63
7) 255 - 110 = 145
8) 298 - 119 = 179

www.ingramcontent.com/pod-product-compliance
Lightning Source LLC
LaVergne TN
LVHW082254070426
835507LV00037B/2293
9781683219460